Originally published in German by Gabriel Verlag.

First English edition published 2016
Printed in USA
22 21 20 19 18 17 16   1 2 3 4 5 6 7 8
ISBN: 978-1-5064-0883-5

Library of Congress Cataloging-in-Publication Data is available

Sparkhouse Family
510 Marquette Avenue
Minneapolis, MN 55402
sparkhouse.org

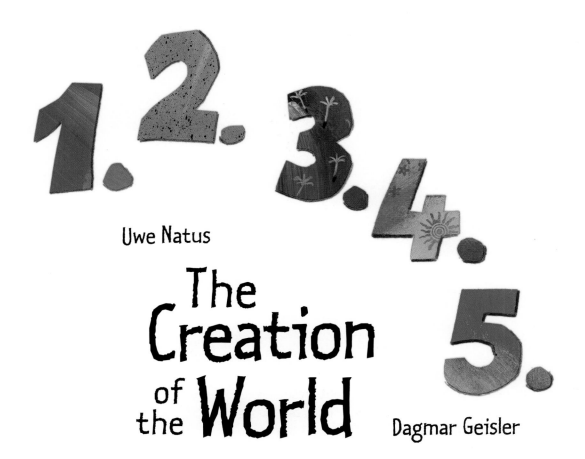

Uwe Natus

The
Creation
of the **World**

Dagmar Geisler

Sparkhouse Family

Minneapolis

The First Day

Before the earth, the stars,
or anything else existed,
there was only quiet,
swirling darkness.

The Spirit of God
hovered there, waiting.

Then—all of a sudden—God said,
"Let there be light!"
and—in a brilliant flash—there was light.

This was God's work
on the first day of creation.

It was very good.

The Second Day

The earth and the skies were hidden
under deep water and thick fog.
Waves crashed against each other
like a fierce storm at sea.

God said, "Let there be space to breathe."

Clouds jumped up to the heavens,
and God named the air above the water, "Sky."

This was God's work
on the second day of creation.

It was very good.

The Third Day

God was only getting started
with the creation.
Next God said:
"Let land appear!"

Towering mountains,
gentle valleys, and long stretches
of sandy beach rose up,
pushed the water aside,
and made dry land.

God planted flowers, trees, and vegetables
in the earth's dark soil and
designed them to make their own seeds
—seeds that fell, nestled themselves into the dirt,
sent down roots, and bloomed, over and over again.

Oak
Maple

Fir
Birch

Beech
White Ash
Elm

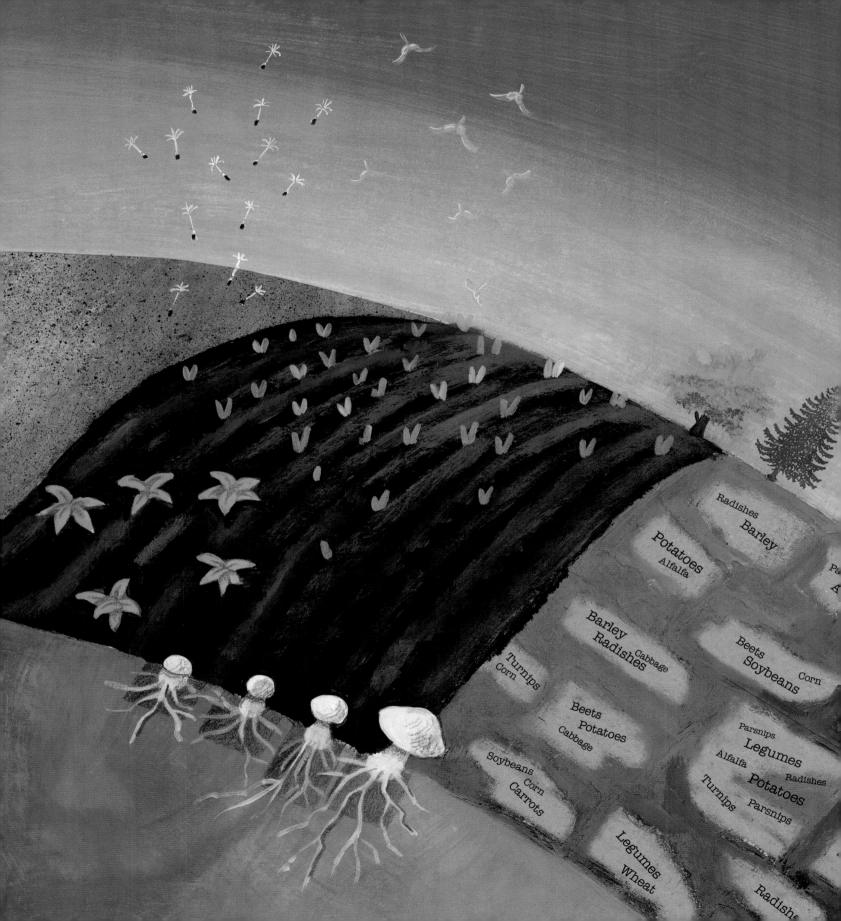

Soon the earth was clothed in beauty.
Yellow sunflowers stood proud on thick,
sturdy stalks.

Pink tulips swayed in the fresh air.
Soft green grasses swept over the hills.

This was God's work
on the third day of creation.
It was very good.

The Fourth Day

The plants needed water and soil from the earth,
but they needed something else, too.
God said, "Let there be two lights in the sky!"
The burning sun and silver moon appeared.

The sun streamed down on the earth during the day,
warming it, helping plants to grown strong and healthy,
and making all of creation shine.

At night, the moon cast a blue glow
over the sleeping land.

Then God scattered handfuls
of twinkling lights around the moon—
these are the stars that still light up the night.

This was God's good work
on the fourth day of creation:

It was very good.

The Fifth Day

Much of the earth was water—
deep blue oceans, rushing green rivers,
and sluggish, muddy streams.

God said, "Let the waters swarm
with living creatures!"

And so they did—Moray eels, dolphins, and
enormous whales appeared in the ocean.
Clams hid in their shells.
Seahorses and seadragons preened and pranced
as crabs scuttled below on the sandy floor.

Then God said,
"Let birds glide
above the earth!"

Suddenly the sky was filled
with flying things:
red-tailed hawks and hummingbirds,
eagles and Eastern bluebirds.
downy woodpeckers and doves,
owls and Orioles.

This was God's good work
on the fifth day of creation:

It was very good.

The Sixth Day

But God still wasn't finished!

God said, "Let there be wild animals and creeping things and beasts of the earth!"

Animals appeared—
quiet giraffes with gangly necks,
patient, hard-shelled tortoises,
joyful, galloping horses,
sneaky red foxes,
careful, tiptoeing meerkats,
and billions of insects that
felt their way along in the dirt.

Then God did the most amazing thing of all.
"Let there be people, made in our image!"

God made two people and told them that
the air was theirs to breathe,
the plants were theirs to eat,
the animals were theirs to care for,
and they were there to love each other.

They were full of gratitude
for all of God's excellent gifts.

This was God's good work
on the sixth day of creation:

It was very good.

The Seventh Day

There was nothing left for God to do—
the work was all done, and
creation was complete!

So God spent the day resting:
watching the clouds move across the sky,
savoring the sweet smell of the flowers,
and listening to the happy chatter of the people
as they sat relaxing in the sun.

And it was very, very good.